CU00651606

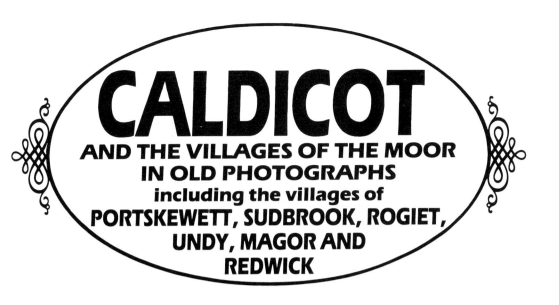

CALDICOT
AND THE VILLAGES OF THE MOOR
IN OLD PHOTOGRAPHS
including the villages of
PORTSKEWETT, SUDBROOK, ROGIET, UNDY, MAGOR AND REDWICK

Volume 1

by Malcolm D. Jones

Foreword by
St. JOHN ROSSLYN GOFF
B.E.M., J.P.

Old Bakehouse Publications

Abertillery

First published in March 1995
Reprinted in February 2000
Reprinted in February 2008

ISBN 1 874538 50 6

Published in the U.K. by
Old Bakehouse Publications
Church Street,
Abertillery, Gwent NP13 1EA
Telephone: 01495 212600 Fax: 01495 216222
Email: theoldbakeprint@btconnect.com
Website: www.oldbakehouseprint.co.uk

Made and printed in the UK
by J.R. Davies (Printers) Ltd.

British Library Cataloguing in Publication Data: a catalogue
record for this book is available from the British Library.

Foreword
by St. John Rosslyn Goff, B.E.M, J.P.

It is with much pleasure that I write this foreword for such a detailed and well documented publication illustrating the area of Caldicot and the villages of the Moor.

I was born in Caldicot in 1926 my father being a 'fireman' on the Great Western Railway and my mother having deep roots in the area. Photograph 10 shows the Old Police Station where my great grandfather lived when he was the constable for this rapidly developing area. I have continued to live in Caldicot and have witnessed first hand, many of the changes that are recorded in this publication, so I am grateful to see these preserved for the future.

Reading through this book has rekindled many memories of my youth and I have seen many photographs that have not been published before. Malcolm Jones is to be congratulated for all the research, dedication, foresight and effort in preserving in a volume such as this, so many facets of the life of the area in this pictorial way.

Future generations will be grateful for the work done by Malcolm Jones; the written word can describe well the affairs of the past and is essential, however, the photographs give an added dimension and show with more realism the conditions of the past, the way in which we have developed, the way in which the people of the locality lived and how they enjoyed themselves.

As you scrutinise the contents of this book you see set out the full panoply of village life in the late 19th century and the early and mid years of this century. This is a living and pictorial proof of life as it was and how things have changed over this relatively short period. It is hoped that today's village and town life will also be preserved in the way captured in this publication.

I offer my sincere congratulations to all involved in this excellent publication and commend it to you.

St. John Rosslyn Goff, B.E.M. J.P.

Introduction

Today, the area between the M4 Motorway and the Severn Estuary is a hive of activity. The population is rising rapidly, villages and towns are expanding and modern hi-tech factories have located here. Yet still, clearly visible all around us are reminders of the region's eventful and fascinating history.

The vicinity covered by this book spans approximately seven miles and embraces seven communities, each with its own character. There is evidence to show that human activity goes back to at least the Neolithic period, with the remains of a barrow (burial site) at Heston Break, Portskewett and continued through the Bronze Age, with the recent find of a portion of a boat at Caldicot Country Park. We do not have to look far for proof of the impact the Romans had on the locality. After their departure we fall into the aptly named 'dark ages'. It is not until the Norman Conquest that the area's history is revived. With their arrival, order is eventually restored to the district and throughout the middle ages, villages settled into a rural farming existence.

In the 12th Century the monks of Goldcliff Priory had set about effectively draining the marshy lands adjoining the Severn Estuary, which we now know as the Caldicot Levels. This was successfully achieved by means of a network of ditches or 'reens' as they are known locally. To this day, these low lying areas are drained by the same system thereby producing rich pasture land.

In 1606 disaster struck the Caldicot Levels - The Great Flood. It reached more than three feet high in places, as shown by a marker recording the water level in Redwick Church. There is also a plaque in Goldcliff Church describing the great loss of life and property.

The next local upheaval was the coming of the railways in 1850 and then the subsequent influx of workers when construction of the Severn Tunnel began in 1879. With the ease of travel and transportation of goods, a small local industrial revolution followed. The Wire Works opened at Caldicot Pill and soon became a major employer in the area. The first half of the 20th Century witnessed a steady but unspectacular growth in population. Scenes illustrated within this book reflect peoples' lives during this period, the background was predominantly agricultural and partly industrial. It was not until the early 1960's that major changes and development occurred. Construction of the new steelworks at Llanwern resulted in the immigration of thousands of steelworkers to the area, many coming from the Welsh mining valleys and some from Swansea and West Wales. By the end of the 1960's Caldicot had a population of more than 7000 people, to many, an unofficial 'new town'. It also changed the other small country villages into the ever growing communities that we see today.

With the opening of the Second Severn Crossing due on the 27th April 1996 yet another unknown and exciting chapter will open for Caldicot and the Villages of the Moor.

It is fortunate for us that the camera arrived in the neighbourhood just before the turn of the century (approximately sixty years after its invention). The tremendously popular Edwardian hobby of postcard collecting flourished, as this has afforded modern-day people a look at village life before everything disappears forever.

I hope this pictorial history will bring back many memories to the more mature reader and enlighten those people who have decided to make this area their home.

I would like to record my gratitude and appreciation to those people who have helped in many ways with the production of this book, especially my family for their patience and support. I must also give extra thanks to my eldest son Richard for his assistance in researching and collating the contents of this publication.

M. D. Jones

Contents

CHAPTER 1

Caldicot

1. A view titled 'The Square Caldicot' 1905. Perhaps the owner of the horse and cart is in the Cross Inn sampling the local brew! The building in the centre was at one time a public house called the Beaufort Arms. The message on the reverse of this postcard refers to the writer having a nice trip across the Severn on the new boat 'The Lady Ismay'.

2. Newport Road, Caldicot 1905. Local people might know Porters shop on the right of the picture. The large Monkey tree on the left adorned the garden of the former Jubilee House.

3. Newport Road, Caldicot in 1921. A sign hangs upon the shop on the left of this scene, reading 'Pride Confectioners'. The group of people on the left consists of Melville Williams, Dolly Gleed, Constance Williams and Leonard Williams.

4. Newport Road, Caldicot 1925, viewed from a little further up the road. William Porter's newsagents and sweet shop is on the right. Also on the right is Jack Porter as a boy, later to become the organist at St. Mary's Church.

5. Newport Road, Caldicot in 1905, still a rural village scene and not a shop in sight! The garden fence on the left belongs to the former Rhyd Cottages, now demolished, which stood where Jubilee Way and Washbournes Garage are today.

6. Newport Road, Caldicot in 1957. A similar scene as above, more than half a century later but little has changed. The same location today looks very different, the Methodist Church being the only building still standing.

7. An early view of the village in about 1900. The roads have yet to be improved and are only slightly better than dirt tracks! The parish council wrote to the County Council in 1902, protesting at the deplorable state of the village roads and requesting that footpaths be kerbed.

8. A similar view as above more than thirty years later. The building on the left became a well known local landmark, 'Mrs. Dally's Sweet Shop.'

9. The White Hart Caldicot in 1905, complete with central illumination and its own law enforcement! The extension on the right of the building was known as 'The Committee Room', where dances, darts matches and such events were regularly held. On the far right of the picture are stables where you could leave your horse whilst staying overnight at The White Hart Hotel.

10. The Cross Caldicot in 1921, from Chepstow Road. The Police Station on the left of the picture is conveniently situated to keep an eye on two of the village inns.

11. Chepstow Road Caldicot 1905, this time looking out of the village from The Cross. Notice the abundance of elm trees on the left of the picture. On the right is the original Caldicot Police Station whilst beyond, is the Bible Christian Chapel.

12. Church Road Caldicot in 1957. The wooden hut on the right began life as the parish hall. From 1941 to 1953 it was the British Restaurant, it was then converted to the Y.M.C.A. Hall.

13. The Cross Caldicot in 1957. The building on the right is the premises of W.J. Evans, Chemist and adjoining are the village public toilets, conveniently situated near the centre of the village.

14. Chepstow Road Caldicot in 1957. The White Hart is still standing, it being 1969 before it was demolished after being declared unsafe. Look closely and you will see that a roundabout has been constructed at The Cross, to cope with an increasing amount of traffic.

15. The Square Caldicot in 1905. The principal form of transport is still the horse and the evidence of this is to be seen on the road, outside Mr. Squibb's Post Office! The advertisement on the window is for a Fete and Gala with a £35 prize for pony racing. A few of the people on this photograph have been identified as follows, left to right: Lucy King, Master Sheppard, Mr. Sheppard, Mr. Sheppard and James King. Unfortunately the author was unable to trace the names of the other three young boys.

16. Newport Road Caldicot in 1905. West End Terrace on the right of this picture has not changed too much, but the left side of the road is completely different. The three stone cottages and Gwillims Farm, just visible behind the tree, have all been demolished.

17. Newport Road Caldicot in 1933. The building on the left is James the saddlers and the houses on the right are Coronation Terrace with the Coronation Stores beyond.

18. Newport Road Caldicot in 1905. Pantile Row is on the left of the picture and the scene is a familiar one today, having changed little.

19. West End Caldicot at around 1910, with Yew Tree Row on the right of the picture and Woodbine Cottages on the left.

20. The Avenue Caldicot. When this photograph was taken in about 1910 these houses were considered to be most opulent. As always the children are only too pleased to pose for the camera.

21. Station Road Caldicot in 1905. The locals knew this area as Ben Acre. The West End Hotel (now Francescas Restaurant) at the top of the hill, has yet to be built.

22. Adams' Shop, London House, Chepstow Road Caldicot in 1905, complete with a splendid pair of lamps outside. Adams's served Caldicot as grocers for many years, including delivery of goods to your door by means of the shop bicycle. The business finally ceased trading on the 30th June 1982.

23. Pool Hill Caldicot around 1930. This area is now known as West End. The gentleman on the horse and cart is Mr. Grimmer delivering the milk. A portion of the wall on the right of the picture is still standing today, behind the telephone box adjacent to Orchard Close.

24. West End during the heavy snow of 1947. Vallis Terrace is on the far left of the picture. The photograph is standing where the Zebra Crossing is situated today.

19

25. An early photograph of workers outside the Welsh entrance to the Severn Tunnel. Wages for working a ten hour day on the tunnel ranged from 1s 8d (8p) for boys to 8s 4d (42p) for foremen, miners earning an average of £1 18s (£1.90) per week and labourers £1 7s 6d (£1.37). At the time, local farm and road workers were earning around a fifth of this. The tunnel opened for regular traffic in 1886 after a chequered 13 year construction period.

26. This 1905 postcard graphically illustrates the amount of material that had to be extracted to create the cuttings, before the construction of the tunnel could begin.

27. Caldicot village, from the church tower in 1957. The original St. Mary's School is in the centre of the picture and beyond, in the background, is the recently completed Caldicot College.

28. A rural scene, Caldicot 1947. On the left is Church Cottage, now having been completely renovated. The timber framed building in the centre of the picture is the former coach house, converted to a private dwelling by Dr. Walford Davies. St. Mary's Church is to be seen in the background.

29. The first Co-op store in Caldicot. It was situated opposite the present site of Wye Valley Studios and later became Miles Boot & Sweet Shop. The boy on the right of the picture is believed to be Harold (Fishy) Davis.

30. Mr. W. James, saddle and harness maker outside his premises that once stood near where the Good Measure public house stands today. He ceased trading in approximately 1938. Advertised on the wall is the Ingersol 5/- watch.

31. The newsagent shop of Mr. Rowland (Roly) Williams, in the mid 1950's. The paper boy pictured is Basil Jenkins.

32. The interior of the above shop. Pictured left to right are Mrs. Raymond, Mr. Roly Williams, Mrs. Williams and Mrs. Baker.

33. Washbourne's Hardware Shop Caldicot, built onto the front of the original Wesleyan Chapel, which had been constructed in 1810. Mr. Cyril Washbourne began the business by selling bicycles, but later added a hardware store (seen here) and also a garage.

34. Caldicot Hall, also called the Great House, built in 1759 by Henry Wise, shipbuilder at Caldicot. It was later owned by the Rev. Edmund Turberville Williams, vicar of Caldicot from 1841 to 1885, who retained it but did not actually live there. On his death in 1903, he left it to Benjamin L. Perry. He in turn, let it to William Mullock and then until 1915 to Mrs. A.M. Lewis. It was then occupied by Col. Godfrey Phillips. From 1935 to 1939 Col. S.L. Cummins lived in Great House which was then called Caldicot Hall and was very active in work for the parish. It was then bought at auction by William Adams. He let it to Henry Mortimer whose family may be seen in this view. William J. Morgan purchased both Caldicot Hall and Church Farm in 1941 and sold part of the land to the Rural District Council and the remainder to a building company. Its site is now occupied by the lower part of Taff Road on the Hall Park Estate, hence the name.

35. Wesley House, which once stood opposite the Methodist Church where Wesley Buildings stand today. This imposing residence had stables, a store and a bake house at the rear and was at sometime occupied by Hubert and his son Rowland Hill.

36. The Firs, Caldicot. This house stood where the Haywain public house stands today. At sometime the property was occupied by the Jones Family, who farmed the nearby land.

37. Pool Cottage, Caldicot (Mrs. Monk's cottage). This once stood on Newport Road opposite its junction with Shakespeare Drive and is seen here in the bleak winter of 1947.

38.   The Old Tippling Philosopher Caldicot, in 1905 when Mr. Rowlands was the landlord. The Castle
Football Team had its headquarters at The Tippling Philosopher during the early part of this century.

39.   Ightfield House Caldicot, better known as The Deepweir Motel, seen here in 1918. The writer
of the original postcard informs us that she is staying here for three days whilst visiting Caldicot.

"CALDICOT, near Chepstow. August 1832"
One of a limited edition of 100 reproductions from the original drawing by an anonymous artist in 1832

40. St. Mary's Church Caldicot from an early line drawing dated 1832.

41. This is the interior of St. Mary's Church taken from a mid-eighteenth century lithograph. The picture shows it prior to the major restoration work which took place during the years 1857-8. The work included new battlements for the towers, a new tower clock, a Staffordshire tiled floor, fine organ and font near the south door. Father Edmund Tuberville Williams, vicar from 1841 to 1885 is to be credited with the restoration plans and much of the total cost of £2000, a sensational sum for the period.

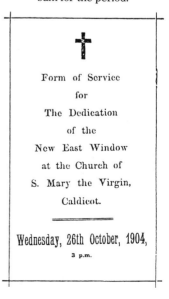

Form of Service

for

The Dedication

of the

New East Window

at the Church of

S. Mary the Virgin,

Caldicot.

Wednesday, 26th October, 1904,

3 p.m.

42. An exterior photograph of St. Mary's taken in the year 1905 and the scene has not changed significantly since. The present building is some 500/600 years old and there is evidence of an even earlier place of worship on this site. The present vicar is the Reverend Peter John Smallman Edwards who has been the incumbent since 1989.

43. St. Mary's Church in 1905. The interior has altered considerably over this century. The decorative plasterwork to the walls, embellished with scriptual texts including the Ten Commandments, have all been removed and the walls pointed. Gone too are the oil lamps and the inner south porch. The rood screen now occupies a different position, the church having been adapted to the needs of modern-day worship.

44. Father Theodore Mansel Rhys Younghughes B.A., vicar of Caldicot 1916 to 1938, with the altar servers in 1936. Father Younghughes died after a tragic accident at the vicarage, when he knocked over an oil lamp which caused fatal burns. He is buried adjacent to the west doorway of the church.

45. Father Younghughes with his churchwardens Dr. Strong, Mr. D.H. Parry and an all male choir in 1936.

46. Father Robert C. Garrod, vicar of Caldicot 1939 to1953, with his churchwarden Mr. D.H. Parry and still an all male choir in 1941.

47. St. Mary's Church Caldicot, choristers in 1942. Left to right: Unknown, Unknown, Don Peppin, Unknown, Ken Williams and John Harries.

48./49. Two photographs of St. Mary's campanologists or bellringers as many of them prefer to be known. The group on the left is seen outside the South porch and the year is approximately 1890. Below is another gathering with the Rev. Frederick W. Clark in the centre. The Rev. Clark served as vicar from 1893 to 1916 and judging from the style of dress, this photograph probably dates from around the year 1910.

During the renovations of 1857-8 as mentioned earlier, attention was paid to the condition of the bells. A new No.4 was provided by a specially levied church rate and Nos. 6 and 7, both dating from the 17th century were re-cast. Father Williams came to the rescue yet again in 1882 by donating four more, Nos. 1, 2, 3 and 5.

50. Caldicot Scouts with the Rev. Frederick W. Clark around 1910. Also at this time the Wesleyan Chapel formed a detachment of the Boys Brigade with a band. The latter proved such an attraction that the boys deserted the Scouts for the Boys Brigade.

51. Caldicot First Company Church Boys Brigade circa. 1906, pictured on Newport Road with the entrance to the Avenue on the left. Mr. Lee is the bandmaster on the left and the boy also on the left with the drum, is George Evans. The boy on the left of the front row is Alfred Evans.

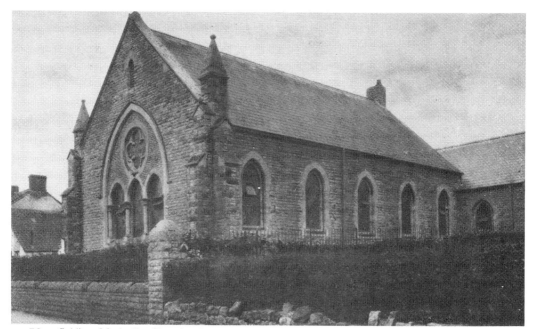

52. Caldicot Methodist Church, photographed during the 1930's and known here as the Wesleyan Methodist Church. The first Wesleyan Chapel in Caldicot was opened in 1807 and was sited on ground now occupied by the pedestrianised shopping centre. John Wesley is recorded as having preached at The Cross in 1741.

53. This is an interior view of the Church and a close look at view of the magnificent organ. The foundation stone for this present Church was laid on May 9th 1895 and the building was opened for worship the following October. The total cost of construction was £1500 of which the sum of £1000 was bequeathed by a Mr. Thomas who was a lay preacher from Ealing, in memory of his wife Alice Dowle of Caerwent. The Church was built predominantly of grey sandstone, donated by Mrs. Cropper of Mount Ballan, daughter of Thomas Walker, builder of the Severn Tunnel. A further donation, was a quantity of yellow sandstone given by Mr. J.R. Cobb of Caldicot Castle.

54. The Methodist Church Carnival and a few of the group have been identified, Burt Barnfield, Ken Margretts, Milly Williams, Wyndham Bald, Grenville Haines, Muriel Williams, Eric Price, Beryl Bald, Mr. Olds (Minister). It was held at Gas Works Lane in 1935. We now know Gas Works Lane as Mill Lane but it terminated near Ash Cottage.

55. Caldicot Methodist Church play around 1937. A few of the cast have been recognised:- Olwyn Owen, Doris Banfield, Barbara Prewett, Joyce Vilday, Dylis Burrows, Will Stanley and Della Arthur.

56. St. Mary's Church School, Caldicot, photographed in 1929 on the retirement of Mr. Blomley. The first school was built in 1847, the cost of construction and the site being borne by the Rev. E.T. Williams, vicar. It was basically a large hall with no separate classrooms. The next incumbent, the Rev. Vernon Collins, decided to fund the cost of adding a separate classroom to the school, to house the infant pupils, this was completed around 1890. By the turn of the century it was necessary to extend the school yet again. The Rev. F.W. Clarke decided to follow the example set by his predecessors and he gave the money required to add three more classrooms to the school. After a long period of service to the village, its status was changed in 1951 when it became 'voluntary aided' and the County Council assumed greater control of its running. In 1955 the senior section of the school moved to the newly opened Green Lane School. The school continued to function for infants only until 1968 when it was replaced by the modern primary school of today. The buildings were demolished a few years later and houses built on the site.

Below is part of the school balance sheet for 1908-9.

I.

Balance Sheet.

July 1st, 1908, to June 30th, 1909.

INCOME.	£	s.	d.
Balance in hand	19	2	6½
Kemey's Charity	5	0	0
Interest, 1907 and 1908 ...		5	7
Subscriptions, as per list ...	8	13	0
	£33	1	1½

EXPENDITURE.	£	s.	d.
Insurance	1	3	3
Printing		7	10
Hedging, Trimming, Cleaning		19	0
Painting, Repairs, Other Work	8	10	9
Ladder, Fixing		14	0
Limewashing, Repairs, Other Work	6	4	10
Gravel, Hauling	3	12	0
Attendance on Medical Officer		5	0
Dinner Time Duty	2	4	0
Balance in hand	9	0	5½
	£33	1	1½

57. Mr. Herbert Blomley, Headmaster of St. Mary's Church School from May 6th 1895 until December 31st 1929. Mr. Blomley also served as peoples' warden of St. Mary's Church from 1902 to 1930. In 1963 a stained glass window depicting the former Church Road School was dedicated to the memory of Mr. H. Blomley and his family. The window is to be found in the St. Brides Chapel of the Church.

58. Headmaster Mr. H. Blomley with his teaching staff in 1914.

59.   Another photograph of Mr. H. Blomley, this time with some of his pupils. The date chalked on the blackboard is October 1914, 3 months into the First World War. The adage of the day was 'The war will be over by Christmas!'

60.   A class photograph of St. Mary's School 1939. Left to right, back row: Unknown, Margaret Jenkins, Unknown, Beryl Gould, Barbara Prewett, Marion Powell, Unknown, Unknown and Unknown. 2nd row: Dorothy Thomas, Unknown, Chick Dowler, Cameron Winter, Dave Thomas, Unknown, Master Rymer, Don Thomas, Unknown, Unknown, John Winter and Marion Peppin. 3rd row: Kitty Williams, Gwyneth Ford, Unknown, Doris Barnfield, Muriel Williams, Hazel Watts, Betty Turner, Isobel Margretts, Unknown and two sisters Misses House. Front row: Master Hodges, Master Scrivens, Roger Williams, Brian Stell, Unknown and Cliff Snook.

61. A group photograph, possibly a school fete in the early 1930's. Left to right, back row: Mr. Phillips, Mr. Smith, Mr. S. Hill, Mr. F. Goff, Mr. W. Margretts, Mr. H. Blomley and Dr. Jones. Front row: Lily Tonkin, Miss Violet Hill, Unknown, Mr. D.H. Parry, Miss E. Blomley, Mrs. Rowe and Miss. E. Younghughes.

62. Teachers and helpers, St. Mary's School Fete in 1933. Left to right, back row: Miss Evans, Molly Pritchard and Miss Johnson. Front row: Unknown, Miss Tonkin, Miss Saunders, Mrs. Jones and Unknown.

63. Headmaster D.H. Parry, surrounded by St. Mary's School dancing team in 1928-1929.

64. Headmaster H. Blomley on the far right, with pupils from St. Mary's School. These allotments, which were tended with care by the pupils, were adjacent to the former school.

65. Caldicot Castle looking from the east in February 1910. This land floods in much the same manner today.

66.   An early photograph of Caldicot Castle before the Eastern Tower of the gatehouse had been renovated by Geoffrey Wheatley Cobb. The Manor of Caldicot was purchased from the Crown in 1857 by one, Charles Lewis and sold to Joseph Richard Cobb in 1885. The Cobb family paid great attention and expense towards the Castle's restoration during their possession until 1963 when ownership was transferred from Lt. Col. Geoffrey W. Cobb, great nephew of Joseph Richard, to Chepstow Rural District Council.

67.   Another early view of Caldicot Castle on this card which was posted at Christmas 1903. It is possible to see the new stone work of the right hand tower of the gatehouse which had recently been restored.

68. The gatehouse of the Castle as seen in 1893 and the gentleman pictured is believed to be Mr. G.W. Cobb responsible for much of the restoration work which rendered the Castle habitable once again after years of neglect. Of the stone built structure, the round keep is the earliest, dating from the 12th Century. Earlier still, are the mound or 'motte' on which it stands and the earthworks which underlie the Castle. The curtain walls and towers were added over a period of some 200 years, the greatest building work being carried out in the 14th Century by Thomas of Woodstock, son of King Edward III. The postern gate is now known as the Woodstock Tower.

69. Clearing the moat on the western side of the Castle in 1913, as part of Geoffrey Cobb's complete renovations. This temporary narrow gauge railway was laid in the moat to facilitate the removal of debris surrounding the Castle. It ran to the rear of the Castle, through the moat embankment and onto the floodplain of the Neddern for disposal.

70. The German field gun which was presented to the village at the end of the First World War. Difficulty and some embarrassment was caused when a home for the gun could not be found and for some time it lay unattended in a ditch close to the Tippling Philosopher. Eventually it was placed upon a base adjoining the Castle drive, by permission of Mrs. Cobb. Here it remained until the Second World War when it was melted down for scrap metal .

71. An aerial view of Caldicot Castle during the 1950's. The residential developments of later years have yet to encroach upon the fields bordering the Castle grounds.

NELSON'S FLAGSHIP FOUDROYANT
WRECKED AT BLACKPOOL 1897.

72.   The original Foudroyant. As well as renovating Castles, Geoffrey Cobb was interested in wooden battleships. In 1892 he purchased from the navy for £6,000, 'The Foudroyant'. She was at one time the flagship of Nelson's fleet and was restored by Cobb at a cost of £30,000. After being refitted and re-rigged, she was sailed around the coastal resorts. Alas, at Blackpool the crew encountered a terrible storm and she was wrecked on Blackpool beach on 16th June 1897.

73.   The new Foudroyant (H.M.S. Trincomalee). After losing his first ship, Cobb promptly set about purchasing another sailing ship and renamed her the Foudroyant. The ship was anchored at Falmouth and was used for the purposes of training young sailors. They frequently visited Caldicot Castle with their band and entertained all present. She is still afloat today and having been launched in 1817, is now the second oldest ship in the world, still afloat. The Foudroyant is now anchored at Hartlepool and undergoing extensive restoration, being a major tourist attraction.

74. The crew of The Foudroyant training ship 1912/13.

75. The funeral of Geoffrey Cobb, of Caldicot Castle in 1931, proceeding from the Castle to the Church. Behind them can be seen the gun which was presented to the village after the first World War.

76. The 1911 Coronation Carnival winding its way along Chepstow Road, towards the village. It is likely that the entrants gathered for the start of the carnival at the Tippling Philosopher.

77. The Coronation of King George V in August 1911 is being celebrated by the crowds at this fete and gala at The Cross organised by the loyal 'Caldicot Castle' lodge.

78. The 1923 village carnival. Amongst others in this entry are believed to be Lewin Ryman, Mr. Stanley, Marjorie Evans, Mr. Dickinson, Mr. Williams, Jack Hale and Francis Cole.

79. Church Pageant 1928. Left to right: Cyril Rowe, Molly Grimmer, Unknown, B. Hooper, Freda Scrivens, Bill Baker and Frank Goff. The Parish Church can be seen in the background.

80. The 1935 Silver Jubilee celebrations. Left to right, back row (standing): J. Stephens, M. Smith, Mr. Payne, D. Parry, C. Meek and B. Dowler. Front row (sitting): Mr. Turner, Mr. Davies, Mr. Goff, Mr. Nancekievill, Mr. Margretts, Mr. Peppin, Sid Hooper, Unknown, Unknown, Mr. Thomas and Mr. Oden.

81. Another picture from the 1935 Jubilee celebrations and ready for the off, in the sack race are, left to right: Mr. Frank Goff, Unknown, Mr. Nancekievill, Unknown, Mr. Oden, Unknown, Mr. Parry, Mr. Smith, the young boy standing second from the far right is Ken Hill. The events are being held on the Church Field and in the background can be seen the former St. Mary's School.

82./83. The Silver Jubilee celebrations of 1935 continue with these two photographs. The one above was taken at the Church Field, unfortunately the author has only been able to trace the name of one of the children, that being Ross Goff who stands on the far right. No doubt however, fellow readers of this book will soom be able to add to this list.

In the lower picture some faces to be seen are Kate Johnson, Mrs. Floyd, Roger Williams, John Adams, Betty Turner and Marion Powell.

84. A young ladies Carnival Group around 1930. Left to right, back row are: Unknown, Oriel Vaughan, Margaret Morgan, Daphne Bolt and Avril Washbourne. Front row: Doreen Arthur and Miss Kathleen Harris.

JUBILEE CELEBRATIONS
OF
KING GEORGE V. and QUEEN MARY
MONDAY, MAY 6th, 1935

FESTIVITIES
FOR THE
PARISH OF CALDICOT

CHURCH SERVICE
FANCY DRESS CARNIVAL, SPORTS, SIDE SHOWS
TEA FOR CHILDREN ATTENDING SCHOOL and
PERSONS 65 YEARS OF AGE AND OVER
THE ROGGIETT AND DISTRICT SILVER BAND
WILL BE IN-ATTENDANCE

WHIST DRIVE
and GRAND CARNIVAL BALL

85. On this Caldicot Carnival float are a few more familiar faces such as Phylis Squibbs, Ethel Bevan, Violet Cooke and Lily Harris. Apologies are expressed to those whom the author has been unable to trace.

51

86. V.J. Day 1945, Station Road, Caldicot. Left to right clockwise: Ethel Bevan, Evelyn Williams, Miss Margretts, Mrs. Margretts, Della Harries, Anne Lane, Kathleen Lane, Mrs. Scrivens, Flo Vaughan, Amy Margretts, Mrs. Tetley, Isobel Titie and Doris Shorey.

87. The 1951 Festival of Britain Carnival, held on the Church Field. Left to right, back row: D.H. Parry, Mrs. Thomas, D. George, A. Evans and Ross Goff. Front row: Pat Day (Festival Queen) and Wendy Hodges.

88.   The playing fields committee. Left to right, back row: Percy Arthur, Bill Stell, Will Williams, Frank Coles and Cyril Washbourne. Front row: David Parry and Mr. Paske (The Gasworks).

89.   It was decided at a public meeting in June 1935 that the village needed a playing field and as there was £43 18s 5d left over from the Silver Jubilee Fund, it was voted that this should go towards the new playing fields. A committee was formed and fund raising continued steadily until 1940 when it was decided to suspend it for the duration of the war. Fundraising activities recommenced in 1946 but it was not until the early 1950's that sufficient monies were available for the purchase of the Longcroft site (£700). In 1954 the first sod was cut by Mr. A.G. Hoare on what is now known as the 'King George V Playing Fields'.

90. The Gymnastic Club. Left to right, Top: Heurtly Harries. Middle: George Winter and G. Merrett. Bottom: John Lewis, Cyril Rowe, Alf Price, Charlie Lewis and Ron Tuckwell. Kneeling: Winch Scrivens.

91. Caldicot Health & Strength Club, around 1940. Left Flag: Grenville Haines, Right Flag: John Harries. Centre boy: Walter Sterry with Ron Tuckwell the instructor on the far left.

92. Caldicot Cycling Club. Left to right, standing: David Hughes, Unknown, Miss Hooper, Eric House and Mr. Thomas. Sitting: Roy Baker, Brian Stell, Unknown, Glyn House, Unknown and Miss Jenkins.

93. Members of the Girls Friendly Society pictured in Newport Road Caldicot in 1955. Left to right are Gwyneth Ford, Joan Whitworth, Barbara Perry, Margaret Morgan, Unknown, Molly Court, Joyce Margretts, Molly Pritchard, Unknown, Betty Turner, Dorothy Thomas, Miss Bush, Jean Price, Pamela Robbins, Joan Davis and Marion Peppin.

94. Caldicot Y.M.C.A. F.C. Presentation Night in 1953. Left to right, back row: Jeff Cullimore, John Barker, Jim Washbourne, Brian Jones, Arthur Burrows, Tony Powell, Dennis Baynton, Wally Sterry and Mel Williams. Middle row: Dave Hodges, Francis Mitchell, Tony Stephens, Alan Collard, Alec Hall, Roger Williams, Pat Bladon and John Harris. Front row: Lionel Bowen, Fred Powell, Jim Dally, Wilf Rosser, Marc Collard, Harold Arm and Horace Curtis.

95. The cast in the 1947 Nativity Play. Amongst others pictured are Marion Woolard, Mrs. Day, Mrs. Turner, Mrs. Squibbs and Mrs. Powell.

96. A group outside the parish hall, on Church Road, possibly in the 1930's. Left to right, standing: Mesdames Davies, Hill, Williams, Boye, Squibbs, Vaughan, Washbourne, Lusty, Williams (of the Pill), Price, Roberts and Baker. Front row: Violet Hill, Mrs. Matthews, Mr. Penry Thomas, Unknown and Mrs. W.C. Jones.

97.   The chorus line from Caldicot Operatic's 1953 production of the Gondoliers. Quite a few faces have been identified, Cyril Rowe, John Mitchell, Pat Bladon, Wilfred Gleed, Queenie Prosser, Mr. H. Curtis, Harry Fincham, Emrys Williams, Bill Turner, Ern Saunders, Roger Williams, Hilda Morgan, Cynthia Brace, Irene Evans, Cassie Curtis, Pam Robbins, Eileen Margretts, Pat Day, Isobel Margretts and Blanche Edwards.

98. On stage is the cast of yet another production by the ever popular Caldicot Operatic Society. Local readers are cordially invited to assist in naming the costumed artistes, amongst whom are John Evans and Jack Nation.

99. Four of the cast from Caldicot Operatic's 1954 production of Iolanthe. Left to right are John Michael, Ann Evans, Cynthia Brace and Pat Bladon.

100. Caldicot Y.M.C.A. Football Team 1948/49 season. Left to right, standing: Wilf Prosser, Unknown, Mr. Roberts, Mr. Hodges, Tichy Brown, Noel Gardner, Bob Simmonds, Brian Richards. Sitting: Keith Collet, Unknown, Unknown, Mr. Jim Washbourne and Colin Harrison. Little boy in the front is Ray Washbourne.

101. A 1933 photograph of a Caldicot youth football club. Left to right, back row: B. Bowen, Heurtly Harries, Joe Harris, Ron Tuckwell, J. Mahoney, Mr. D. Parry (Headmaster), Ron Scrivens and D. Jones. Middle row: L. Carter, H. May, G. Pritchard, A. Squibbs and W. Rowlands. Front row: B. Barnfield and R. Nancekievill.

102.   Regrettably only two names are known on this 1950's Caldicot Football Team. They are, Roy Baker and Jim Washbourne.

103.   1951 Festival of Britain. The Castle Inn darts team. Back row: Harry Mortimer, Pat Mahoney, Frank Compton, Bill Mahoney, Bernard King and Reg Macey. Middle row: Jim Harding (senior), Alec Dodd, Doug Baynham and Jim Smallcombe. Front row: John Dickenson, Jim Harding, Bill Dodd, Norman Savory and Bill Bartram.

104. Caldicot R.F.C. Under 16's Season 1992/93.

Left to right, back row: Mike Hobbs (Coach), Adam Duckett, Kier Harding, Stephen Jones, Charles Heaven, Paul Downing, Ian Hobbs, Paul Rudd, Brian Hallsworth, Jonathan Blaydon, Lee Westerman and Gary Ellis (Coach). Front row: Michael Davis, John Cadogan, Nathan Jones (Vice Captain), Joel Rees, Ryland Griffiths (Captain), Kevin Wadely, Laurence Sealy, John Wayne Hughes and Ben Baker.

Portskewett

105.   The ancient parish church of St. Mary the Virgin photographed in 1905. The church registers date back to 1593, but the building itself is much older, being of Norman origin.

106.   The interior of St. Mary's Church in 1933. The internal view is much the same today, except that a change in power source has led to the removal of the oil lamps.

107.   The village stocks 1920. They were erected in 1850 and once stood on the grass verge outside the churchyard. The stocks are now in Chepstow museum, having been moved there some years ago for their preservation.

108.   The War Memorial photographed in 1920 on the occasion of its unveiling on November 13th of that year. The following names are engraved on the memorial in remembrance of those who made the ultimate sacrifice.

1914-1918 War
Bert Beasley, Audley Blight, Daniel James Donovan, Jeremiah Donovan, Charles Drower, Ernest Evans, Albert Gardner, Frederick Gardner, Albert James Hale, Archie Harris, Ernest Humphreys, George Humphreys, Thomas King, William King, George Morse, Edward Pickering, William Spencer, Harry Waters, Tom Ernest Webb M.M., Owen Williams and Albert Edward Richings.

1939-1945 War
Muriel Perry, Frederick Boon, Albert R. Clutterbuck, William F. Edwards, Thomas J. Fieldhouse, Thomas Hayward, Leonard R. Sparks, William C. Wallace and Samuel C. Hughes.

109. Portskewett School and Hotel 1905. There are records of a school existing in Portskewett as early as 1673. The present school building dates from 1871 and is still in use today.

110. School House, Portskewett in 1906. This building adjoins the school (above) and was also constructed in 1871.

111. An early class photograph of Portskewett School. Judging by the appearance of the pupils' clothes - boys' high neck collars and the small children in the front row with their long lace up boots, this photograph probably dates from around the turn of the century.

112. A class photograph of Portskewett School in 1932. Left to right, back row: John Woods, Billy Blight, Lance Sparks, Master Mundy, Albert Reece, Ronnie Grace, Unknown, May Roberts, June Thomas, Roy Williams and Ralph Hudd. Front row: Trevor Waters, Cliff Williams, Lyn Andrews, Francis Williams, Mary Wakley, Doreen Woods, Brenda Noise, Dulcie Thomas and Bessie Harris.

113. Portskewett School in 1931. Some of the following pupils have been identified: Francis Williams, Lilian Haigh, Ada Davis, Ron Grace, Jim Foster, Billy Blight, John Greening, Raymond Hart, Jean Sirrell, Edith Sparks, Hubert Reese, Sadie Pearce, John Leonard, Ronnie Chappel, Olive Brown, David Grimmer, Spencer Wood, Jane Thomas, Ken Replie, Lance Sparks, John Woods, Debbie Thomas, Doreen Woods, Trevor Waters, Mary Edwards, Ossie Sirrell, Bill Thomas, Eric Gipp, Helen Webb, Dolly Davis, Mervyn Humphries, Lionel Cocks, Pat Gipp and Betty Tuck.

114. A Portskewett School photograph from 1930 and the pupils are left to right, back row: Doreen Leonard, Monica Feltham, June Thomas, Joyce Alexander, Olive Brown, Doreen Woods, Lynne Andrews, Vera Newcombe and Dolly Davis. Front row: Mary Edwards, Sadie Pearce, Betty House, Lillian Hauge, Francis Williams, Edith Sparks, Joan Greening and Jean Hudd.

115. The year on this occasion is 1932 and pictured left to right are, back row: Llean March, Louise Parker, Edith Sparks, Francis Williams, Mary Roberts, John Cherington, Vera Newcombe and Ben March. 2nd row: Ethel Folks, Doreen Watkins, Ruth Shepard, Unknown, May Roberts, Betty Evans, Unknown and Unknown. 3rd row: David Sperrin, Unknown, Jimmy Farmer, Bob Parry, Lionel Hudd, Michael Foster, Unknown, Wendy Hutchins, Linda Folks. Front row: Reg Hadaway, Andrew Harding, Unknown, Unknown, Billy Blight, Unknown, John Major and Unknown.

116. Portskewett School football team 1931/32. Left to right, back row: Hubert Reece, Jim Foster, Ron Chapel, Ernie Humphries, Sidney Thomas and Percy Waters. Middle row: John Greening, Oswald Sirrell and Alan Richards. Front row: David Grimmer and Charlie Pearce.

117. Portskewett garden fete 1936. The young girls in the dancing team are, left to right: Mary Counsell, Bronwyn Hopkins, Jean Foster, Joy House, Ann Parker, Helen Webb, Betty Tuck, Audrey Alliston, Dolly Davis, Mary Leonard, Olive Hopkins and Mary Spencer.

118. Portskewett House photographed in 1906. This grand residence was built by Charles Lewis in 1830. It was later occupied by the Lysaght family, owners of the well known Newport steel works. It looks much the same today except that the conservatory has since been demolished.

119. The Walker Memorial Home was owned by Doctor and Mrs. Cropper of Mount Ballan and was used as an orphanage, but on the outbreak of the First World War in 1914 it was converted to a Red Cross Hospital. By November of that year it had its first patients, twelve Belgian soldiers. By June of 1916 this had been increased to fifty patients. All the wounded were regularly entertained in the local villages with lantern slide shows and musical recitals etc. and even taken to Newport to see the pantomime at Christmas. The building was demolished on instructions from Mrs. Cobb, who complained that it had interfered with her view from the Castle! The foundations can still be seen today on the left hand side of the Chepstow Road, just above the Mitel roundabout.

120.   Looking towards the Crick Road from Main Road in 1907, with Manor Farm on the right of the picture, obscured by trees. An idyllic scene, clearly showing that around the turn of the century, the Main Road led towards Crick and not Caldicot.

121.   Main Road looking towards Caldicot in 1905. The long building, half way down on the right of the photograph was the Blacksmith/Undertaker's at one time kept by Tom Crook. The photographer could afford to stand in the middle of the road without fear of motorised traffic in this sleepy little village.

122. A very early photograph of Main Road, Portskewett looking towards Chepstow. The only house to be seen is 'Pinespits'. It is believed that the house is so called, because centuries ago it was the practice to haul boats to this spot in order to pitch their undersides, prior to refloating.

123. Main Road, Portskewett in 1930. The photographer is standing just below Blackrock Road, looking towards Caldicot. The three pairs of semi-detached house on the right were built by Mr. Richards of Crick in 1927.

124. A group of small children stand outside the gardens of Laburnum Terrace, soon after the houses were built by Mr. Sheppherd in 1905.

125. Fields and wide open spaces surround Laburnum Terrace seen here in 1905. The two children are heading down Station Road. The scene today is totally transformed and occupied by housing development.

126. This busy little industrial scene is of Portskewett Sawmills at Station Road and was photographed in the year 1950.

PORTSKEWETT

CHEPSTOW. MON.

Bought of **JOHN WILLIAMS,**

Wholesale and Retail Oil Merchant.

127. Chepstow Rural District Council, proceeding along Main Road, Portskewett in 1959. At the front is the late Thomas Birbeck, the man responsible for recording a great deal of Caldicot's history.

128. The original Portskewett Station that once stood near the Sudbrook railway bridge, which can be seen in the background.

129. A view of the new Portskewett Station, this one showing the branch line to Black Rock and the ferry. In the past, Royal trains would use this siding for their overnight stop. Members of the Royal family and notable politicians, such as Sir Winston Churchill are said to have stayed here.

130. The Black Rock Railway Bridge 1920. The railway to Black Rock and the ferry, was closed and dismantled shortly after the opening of the Severn Tunnel, which rendered the ferry redundant.

CHAPTER 3

Sudbrook

131. The Old Chapel, Sudbrook, in 1904. Correctly 'Holy Trinity', Sudbrook, the church is now a rapidly deteriorating ruin, having been abandoned in the mid-eighteenth century. The last interment was in 1757, that of Blethin Smith a Sea Captain.

132. The Institute, Sudbrook in 1904. Although this postcard is captioned 'The Institute' this building was originally constructed as the Infirmary, complete with a general ward and separate wards for children and females. It also had its own operating room and mortuary. Seen below is a copy of the original plans for the Infirmary.

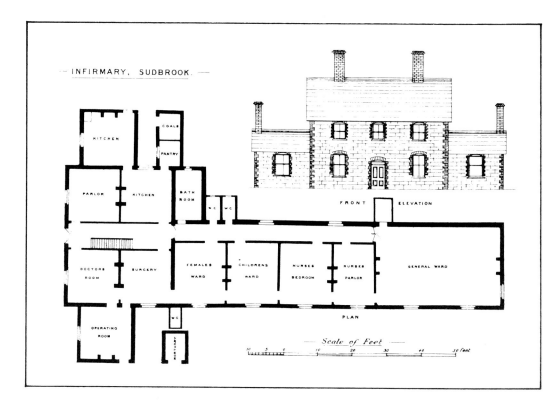

133. A class photograph of Sudbrook Council School in 1914. Regrettably the author has been unable to trace any names on this occasion.

134. A traditional class photograph of Sudbrook Council School in 1923. The Headmaster on the right of the picture is Mr. Sedley.

135. A village scene, Sudbrook in 1904. Stone Cottages on the left, were built for the workmen of the Severn Tunnel and were completed by 1882. The villas on the right of the picture were built for the managers and were completed by 1880. The milkman doing his round is purported to be 'Milky Jones from Mathern'.

136. A closer view of Stone Cottages, Sudbrook looking in the opposite direction to the photograph above. Again, the scene is from the mid 1900's.

137. An ivy-clad Post Office Row Sudbrook, in 1904. The Post Office was opened in 1881. Just visible in the background is the former 5 mile 4 chains pumping station.

138. Sea View, Sudbrook in 1904. These houses were built between 1882-1884 for a family and up to six labourers, employed for the construction of the Severn Tunnel.

139. Camp Road Sudbrook in 1904 was completed by 1880. The large water tower has now been demolished.

140. A general view of Sudbrook in 1904. The railway in the centre of the photograph was built to take coal supplies to the Pumping Station, to feed the boilers. These powered the Cornish Beam Engines, which pumped the spring water out of the tunnel. The building on the right was Marshall's Stores, responsible for publishing many postcards of Portskewett and Sudbrook during the first quarter of this century.

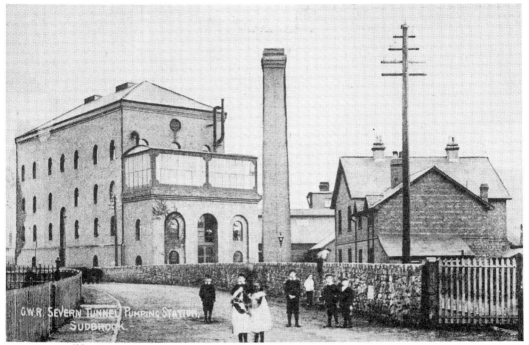

141.   Sudbrook Pumping Station in 1904. This was built to house the massive Cornish beam engines which were brought here to control the great spring that flooded the tunnel headings in 1879 and which still flows today. Children have gathered for this photograph, probably from the adjacent school.

142.   Sudbrook Ship Yard in 1904, which had been created by T. A. Walker after the completion of the Severn Tunnel, in order to make use of his idle workshops. The shipyard constructed mainly small steamers and the largest ship ever built here was the 'Frensham' at 739 tons. After Walker's death the yard was managed by the executors of his estate until 1902. Ownership then passed to Charles Walker until its closure in 1922.

143. The former pumping station at 5 miles 4 chains, which stood opposite Marine Terrace. It has now been demolished.

144. Pumping Station Workmen in 1930. A few of the men have been identified as follows, back row: Jack Jacobs, Bill Edwards, Jack Gardner, Mr. Hicks, Mr. Slayne, Les Edwards and Unknown. Front row: George Powell, Ted Tuck, Joe Devlin, Les Edwards, Edgar Lewis and Lew Coles.

145. Sudbrook pulp mill workers in 1958. Left to right, back row: Tom Stowe, Norman Arnold, Glyn Hazel, Len Waters, Pat Bladon, John Vitte, Doug Jenkins, Gerry Jackson, Fred Chesterman, Les Howells, Phil House, Albert Vaughan, Dave Stocke, Bob Scott and Tony Hudson. Front row: Pete Coles, Les Watkins, Eric Hunt, Glyn Lovell, Doug Lewis, Jock McShane, Walter Cook, Rowland Edwards, Eddy Dimmock, Tom Wilshire, Eddy Lovell, Len Rutten and Alec Harrison.

146. The Camp Portskewett in 1909. Although known as Portskewett camp, it was actually sited at Sudbrook beyond the Roman camp. It was first used as a training camp in the 1880's by the Monmouthshire Artillery Volunteers. Up until the First World War, it was used for live firing practice over the mud flats. With the formation of the Territorial Forces in 1908, other Welsh and English artillery regiments came to use the facilities. The photograph shows the 1st Caernarvon Royal Garrison Artillery Volunteers on their second camp in 1909.

147. Tradition dictates that when a commander's horse dies, it must be buried with a full military ceremony. Here is such an occasion at Portskewett camp in 1909.

148. An unidentified group of soldiers at Portskewett camp pose for the camera. Little do they realise that soon they will be fighting the war to end all wars. (The Great War 1914-1918).

149. Sudbrook Institute R.F.C. 1912/13. Left to right, back row: H.J. Cane, J. Brown, Geo. Beasley, J. Webb and W. Friskney. 2nd row: F. Kicke, W. Farmer, W. Spencer, J. Morse, A. Gardener, W. Davis, A.E. Davis, A.D. Orum, H. Slayne, H.J. Lewis and J. Gardener. 3rd row: T. Pearce, F. Drower, T. Donovan, F. Gardener, C. Pearce, F.S. Morgan, Sid Beasley, S. Windsor and W. Fuller. Front row: E.G. Williams, C. Gardener, R.H. Beasley and Bert Beasley.

150. The Rocks beyond the Roman camp at Sudbrook in 1910. Two young ladies in hats and full length skirts are enjoying the sea air. With the completion of the Second Severn Crossing this view will never look the same again.

151. A gigantic whale which was washed ashore at Sudbrook in 1925. The gentleman standing on the whale is purported to be George Watkins.

152. An advertisment illustrating some of the amenities available at the Black Rock Hotel. The former Black Rock pier is shown in the background.

153. The Black Rock Hotel before the disastrous fire of 1948 which caused much damage. At one time a cattle market was held here and Bristol butchers would come over on the ferry to purchase prime Monmouthshire cattle. The hotel was demolished about twenty years ago.

154. An aerial photograph of Sudbrook pulp mill shortly after its opening in 1958. The building at the top right hand corner is the now demolished pumping station at 5 miles 4 chains.

155. The Mission Hall, Sudbrook in 1904. This was the second such hall, the first one having burnt down in November 1882, soon after it was built. This replacement hall was constructed in less than three weeks. It stood opposite the Pumping Station, but has now been demolished.

CHAPTER 4

Rogiet

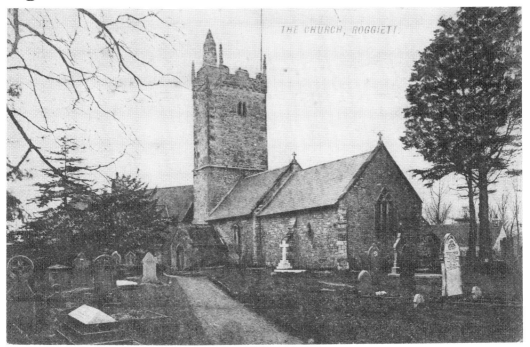

156. St. Mary's Church, Rogiet about 1906. This particular postcard was published by Mrs. Tinham who ran Rogiet Post Office. The Church is situated on the outskirts of the village and dates mainly from the 13th Century. The original dedication was to St. Hillary.

157. The interior of St. Mary's Church in 1933, little unchanged today. The development of Rogiet into a major railway centre in 1887 with the building of Severn Tunnel Junction, resulted in a considerable rise in population. Consequently, the Church was extended in 1903 when a North aisle was added to the Nave.

158. A class photograph of St. Mary's School Rogiet in 1937. Most of the names have been identified and reading from left to right are: B. Macilroy, D. Fry, C. Jones, D. Hill, I. Edwards, N. King, V. Bolton, I. Gazzard, M. Smith, J. Barnet, J. Sims, H. Bluett, M. Bryan, P. Heal, P. Lane, M. Bailey, B. Perrot, P. Andrews, G. Pritchard, Glyn Davis, I. Young, G. Williams, G. Griffiths, I. Kibbey, J. Smith, M. Powell, F. Prior, D. Cheeseman, J. George, D. Lewis, G. Jackson, B. Clemo, H. Sellwood, J. Oliffe, M. Chislett, A. Hawker, J. Hutchings, J. Morgan, W. Poulson, H. Coleman, G. Jackson, J. Treloar, I. Parry, K. Monelle and R. Counsell.

159. St. Mary's Church in Wales School, about 1906. The school was built in 1886 on land given by Lord Tredegar and stood on the opposite side of the road to the present school, where St. Mary's Crescent stands today.

160. The Rogiet Hotel in 1904, the lease of which was signed over by Lord Tredegar in 1888 to the Severn Tunnel Junction Market and Hotel Company Ltd. The market was situated behind the Hotel. The stone barn visible in front of the trees, dates from at least 1797 and was part of the market. The market was held fortnightly on Mondays, for the sale of cattle, sheep and pigs. The tall house on the right was Cartwrights Bakery and is still a bakery today, run by the North family.

161.   A general view of Rogiet as it looked in about 1920 when viewed from the railway bridge over the G.W.R. main line to London.

162.   New Road, Rogiet, now known as Crossway, seen here in 1933 shortly after construction was completed.

163. Monmouthshire & Rogiet Councillors at Rogiet Playing Fields in 1947. Left to right, standing: W.H. Jones, Ken Vincent, Mrs. G. Day, K. Gethin, N. Norton, W. Watkins, F. Grainger and D. Coleman. Sitting: P. Gwillam, J. Gibbon, Mrs. E. Sparks, Sidney Jones, Ernest Jones and T.J. Jones.

164. Station Road Rogiet as seen around 1910, when the total population of the village numbered only 138! The houses on the right of the picture are known as Sea View and were built in 1888 by the Great Western Railway Co.

SEVERN TUNNEL JUNCTION STATION.

165./166.   The Central Platforms of the Great Western Railway Station at Severn Tunnel Junction. The year of this photograph is 1905 and the train standing at the platform has just arrived from the direction of Newport. Note the quaint old gas lamp standards, a once so familiar sight on our railway stations, to be remembered by our more mature readers and railway travellers perhaps? Below is the coaling stage at Severn Tunnel Junction, pictured at the end of the steam era in 1960.

167. A car-carrying train has just arrived at Severn Tunnel Junction. When this service ceased to operate in 1966, the cost of transporting a car through the tunnel was a mere 17 shillings (85p).

168. Severn Tunnel Junction, looking west as seen in 1961. The marshalling yards were opened in 1887, enlarged in 1930, modified in 1960 and closed in 1987. They were previously a valuable source of employment to local people.

169. Great Western Railway employees from Severn Tunnel Junction, enjoying a trip to Cheddar in about 1920. Left to right: W.H. Margretts, W. Titler, Lew Rymer, L. Baker, A. Joyner, Len Slade, Sid Baker, Cyril Hill, S. Collett, B. Holway, N. Offer and Ern Perry.

170. A group of Severn Tunnel railwaymen amongst others are Wilf Lewis, Jack Cook, Alan Squibbs, Reg Lewis, 'Tinny' Thomas, Arthur Turley, Mr. Perryman, Mr. Williams and Mr. Counsell.

171. The G.W.R. Social and Educational Union Choir - Severn Tunnel Junction in the Operetta 'Pearl and the Fishermaiden' in 1925. A few members of the cast have been identified from this early production: Teddy Thomas, Jock Jones, Gwen John, Billy Lines, Miss Ada Hawthorn, Violet Sparks, Dorothy Hancock, Iris Bevan, Gus Bevan and Charlie Hughes.

172. Rogiet and District Operatic Society's 1937 production of San Marino. A few people have been identified as follows: Queenie Prosser, Mrs. Workman, Iris Gleed, Doris Coles, Gladys Dumphy and Violet Hill.

173. Birthday honours for Mrs. E. E. Sparks also celebrating '50 Years in the Labour Movement' in 1947. A few of the group have been identified, these are Mr. Murphy, Mr. Hurst, Fred Walker, Alice Watkins and Mrs. Gardiner. As a thanksgiving for her contribution to local politics, a development of Old Age Pensioners bungalows in Rogiet were built in the 1970's and named Elizabeth Sparks Close.

CHAPTER 5

Undy

174. Undy Wesleyan Chapel in 1908. The postcard is of the stone laying ceremony for the addition of the schoolroom in 1908. The total cost of the construction of the schoolroom amounted to £365, a phenomenal amount at the time, how inflation has taken its toll!

175. The laying of the foundation stone of the schoolroom, at Undy Wesleyan Chapel in 1908. The writer of this postcard says 'I am working at this Wesleyan Chapel'.

176. Undy Wesleyan Chapel in 1907. The chapel was originally built in 1856 at a cost of £177! Judging from this picture, the main road would appear to be in a very poor state of repair. The Chapel closed in the late 1970's and has now been converted into a private dwelling.

177. An early photograph of St. Mary's Church Undy, taken prior to the restoration of the building in the late 1870's. Unfortunately the restoration was rather thorough and involved the removal of the tower, the rebuilding of the nave (with the exception of the west wall), the insertion of new windows throughout and the addition of a vestry to the north side of the chancel.

178. St. Mary's Church Undy in 1906. Compare this photograph with the earlier one above and the alterations made during the Victorian 'restoration' of the building are plain to see. Gone is the unusual tower, replaced by a rather oversized bell-turrett. However, the building retains several original features, including a Norman font, a Norman doorway and a thirteenth century chancel arch.

179. Main Road Undy in 1905. The houses on the left of the picture were known as Morgans Terrace, after Mr. Morgan the builder, who was responsible for their construction. Unfortunately, Morgan went bankrupt and the terrace was never completed. The house on the left in the foreground, was owned by Mr. Fred Read, the local baker.

180. The portable cider mill at Little Hill Farm Undy, where Arlington Close stands today. This ingenious device visited many local farms to crush the cider apples. Pictured left to right are: H.J. Hodges, A.E. Hodges, Joe Simpson, Arthur Thomas, Will Marsden, Harry Bird, Charles Davis and Arthur Bird.

181. The Crossroads Undy in 1910, where the Main Road intersects Vinegar Hill and The Causeway. The seat on the grassy road island is believed to have been erected to commemorate Queen Victoria's Jubilee.

182. Another view of The Crossroads Undy, this time some twenty five years later in 1935. Signposts have now been erected and a new bungalow has been built. Today, this is a busy and at times, dangerous junction.

183.   Undy Halt, pictured here on Easter Sunday 1961. The locomotive is No. 4971 'Stanway Hall'. The halt was opened in September 1933 and closed in November 1964.

CHAPTER 6

Magor

184. Magor Church porch in 1905. The large north porch of Magor Church is of two storeys, access to the upper storey being gained by a staircase from inside the Church nave. There is evidence that this upper room was originally used as the village schoolroom and it still retains its essential fireplace! Notice also the elegant young lady, in contemporary dress, sat upon a convenient tombstone!

185. St. Mary's Church in 1935. The Church was richly rebuilt in the middle ages, which may be explained by its close monastic connections with the Cistercian Abbey at Tintern. The building was much restored in 1868 by the then vicar, Rev. Arthur Saunders when the dedication was changed to St. Mary the Virgin.

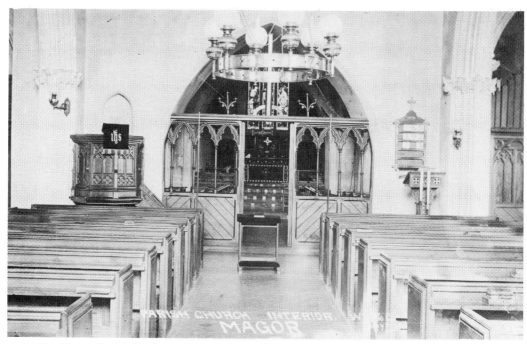

186. Magor Church interior in 1905. An internal view of the Church showing many of the features of its 1868 restoration. A number of these features such as the large hanging lamps and screen have since been removed, the latter during the 1950's. The writer of this postcard says 'This is the Church where I am going to get married'.

187. Ebenezer Baptist Chapel Magor in 1904, prior to the addition of the distinctive roof vents and the insertion of an extra window modifications which were undertaken in 1905.

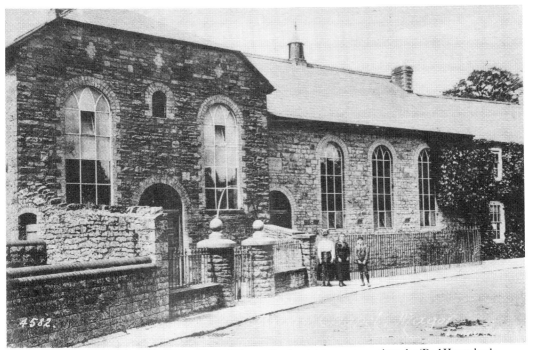

188. The Baptist Chapel in 1922. The building on the far right was at one time the 'Red House' pub.

189. Magor Village viewed from the Church tower in about 1905. Notice beyond the square, open fields, where today large sprawling housing estates exist.

190. A general view of Magor village some 90 years ago but actually photographed from Mill Common Undy, which today is the location of a modern housing estate. Barns and haystacks near the centre of the village, testify to Magor's existence as an agricultural community until fairly recently.

191. The Wheatsheaf Inn 1925, with the landlord Mr. F. Chave and his wife pictured standing in the doorway. Note the water trough under the chestnut tree, refreshment for your horse whilst you enjoy the refreshment at the bar of The Wheatsheaf!

192. Cross Farm Magor, pictured in 1957, which stood almost opposite The Wheatsheaf. Older residents of Magor may remember that Mr. Bill Brace lived here at sometime. The property was demolished in the 1960's and the site is today occupied by 'The Chestnuts', a complex of old age pensioners bungalows.

193. Magor Vicarage seen here in 1906. The property was built in 1861 for the Reverend Arthur Cardinal Saunders, vicar of Magor and Redwick and was designed by John Norton a London architect. It still serves as the vicarage today.

194. Chapel Terrace Magor as seen in the year 1906. This row of houses was owned by Ebenezer Baptist Chapel, hence the name Chapel Terrace and they served the community as almshouses. The much smaller house at the end of the row and on the left of this photograph was however part of the Tredegar Estate.

195. Undy Road 1922, with 'The Wheatsheaf' on the left, proudly proclaiming 'George's bottled beers'. Also on the left sitting on the motorcycle, is Lyn Williams as a young boy. The road surface, rather rough and ready is typical of the district some 70 years ago.

196. 'Mill Common', states this postcard, but this road has been variously described over the years on different postcards as, High Street, Undy Road and Mill Pond Road. This photograph was taken around 1925. The imposing house, centre right of the picture was at one time the Magor Police Station.

197.   George Bolas' garage in 1957. A previous proprietor was Roy Allen. A 'Shell & B.P. Service' are offered. 'The Wheatsheaf' on the right of the picture was at the time selling Hancock's ales.

198.   Newport Road Magor about 1920. The house on the left of the scene is Magor Vicarage and that in the centre is Magor Court. The Vicarage and The Court seem to have been built at a considerable distance from the original village, although the route is now a scene of later housing development.

199. West End Magor pictured in 1935. At this time no houses had, as yet, been built on the left side of the road.

Station Road. Magor. Mon.

200. Station Road Magor in about 1910. The photographer is looking towards The Square and has his back to West End. The fingerpost is pointing right, towards The Station and to Redwick. The building on the right of the street was The Church House Inn, which was at one time described as the counties finest small tudor house. It was demolished in 1965 but the fireplace, tiny windows and staircase were left standing and can be seen today, at the entrance to the car park. A priceless screen and several ancient beams and joists, from the same building were removed to The Cross Inn at Caldicot. Today this is a very different scene, a road passing across the foreground of this location.

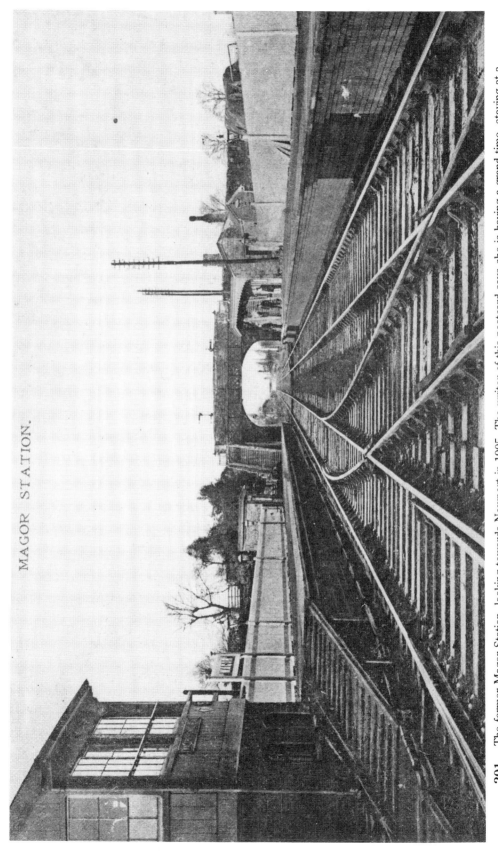

MAGOR STATION.

201. The former Magor Station, looking towards Newport in 1905. The writer of this postcard says she is having a grand time, staying at a farmhouse by the sea. Magor Station closed to passengers in November 1964 and to goods traffic in 1965. Local pressure upon the authorities to re-open the station, has so far proved unsuccessful.

202. Magor Post Office in 1904 and only a solitary oil lamp stands in the middle of the square. Today this area seems to be permanently filled with parked cars!

203. Magor Square in 1905 from a different viewpoint. The post office is on the right of this photograph and was at this time kept by J. Griffiths. In the background can be seen Dorset House, which now houses the doctors surgery.

204. The Square in 1911 and a group has gathered to pose for the camera! Amongst others are, on the left, Curly Williams landlord of 'The Lion' and Walter Bushel is standing next to him. Also present are Ivy Allen and Mrs. Blackaby.

205. The Square in 1906. The building on the right is W.G. Wellingtons' corn & flour store, whilst in the centre is H. Allen's general store, an establishment which was responsible for publishing local postcards. Magor House on the left of the picture remains largely unchanged today.

206.   The Llangybi Hunt, photographed at Magor Square on the 4th February 1910. This postcard was sent only 11 days after the event, demonstrating the speed in which postcards were produced.

207.   The GLOG hounds on the 15th February 1910 in the square. The huntsmen and their pack came by train from Pontypridd, possibly at the invitation of Lord and Lady Rhondda who lived at Llanwern House.

208. The Mill Pond in 1906. The house which can be seen on the left is Pond Cottage which now stands adjacent to the busy Main Road at its junction with Dancing Hill. The writer of this postcard says she is having a jolly time in Magor!

209. Another view of the Mill Pond and seen here are Hunt Brothers and Williams saw mills, where Cliff Morgan's garage stands today. The pond drove a waterwheel which in turn provided power for the sawmills.

210. A busy Magor blacksmith's shop some 90 years ago. The proprietor was Henry Allen and the premises stood adjacent to the square, almost opposite the Baptist Chapel. This postcard was sent to Rose Villa now known as The Rose Inn, Redwick.

211. A Magor Church ladies group photographed probably during the 1920's.

212. A Magor Church School photograph of 1933. Left to right, back row: Miss Mary Keight, Miss Iris Bevan, Reginald Hunt, Leslie Friend, Eric Brenchley, Harold Cochrane, Arthur Kent, Glyn Webb, Bob Sheppard, Ronald Ford, Gordon Friend, Cyril Watkins, Dennis Jones, Philip Wood and Mr. Cliff Lewis. 3rd row: Kitty Read, Mary Waters, Doris Wogan, Kathleen Avery, Ivy Jones, Phyllis Reese, Nora William, Renee Weaver, Dilys Evans, Phyllis Ford, Mary Sheppard, Muriel Hill, Margery Baker, Margery Ford, Fred Brenchley, Jack Cochrane and Doris Ford. 2nd row: May Williams, Mostyn Lawrence, John Gillard, Gwyn Williams, Raymond Cochrane, Harold Chamberlain, John Lewis, Alfred Reese, David Rollings, John Reese, Brynley Waters, Harold Watkins, Bill Sheppard, Roy Hardwick and Mary Partridge. Front row: Ivy Wogan, Nancy Williams, Barbara Kent, Fred Baker, Bill Williams, Morris Cox, Clyde Webb, Grace Brenchley, Joan Reese, Brenda Ware, Pearl Holt, Biddy Wood, Arthur Harris and Tom Baker.

213. 'Dad's Army', 2nd Battalion Monmouthshire Home Guard, 26th Platoon (Magor & Undy) G. Company. This photograph was taken in Undy church hall in December 1940. Left to right, back row are: Bob Brace, Gordon Smith, Philip Wood, Trevor Pritchard, Arthur Kent, Ray Parry, Geoff Atlewell, Harry Phillips and Joe Champion. Middle row: Graham Webb, Lambert Bird, Reverend Thomas Leysham, John Lewis, Bill Reece, Unknown and Charles Smith. Front row: Tom Brenchley, Ron North, Harry Williams, Bill Lines, Dennis Price and Trevor Harris.

214. The Coronation celebrations of King George VI in May 1937. A large crowd has gathered outside the post office and amongst those present are George Ford, Charlie Powell, Roger Adams and Harry Williams.

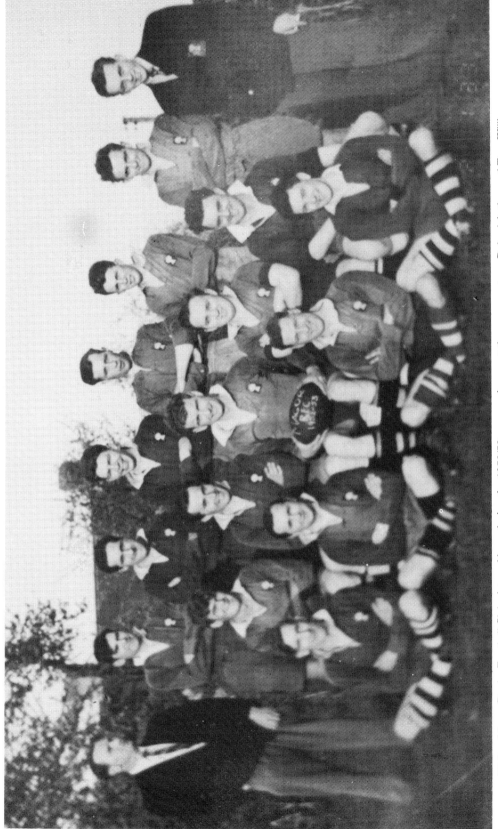

215. Magor Rugby Football Club pictured here during the 1952/53 season. Amongst those present are Roland Arthur and Tom Williams.

CHAPTER 7

Redwick

216. St. Thomas's Church and School, Redwick in 1905. Yet another Church where the patron saint has been changed, as at the neighbouring churches of Magor and Rogiet. Redwick Church has been recorded with three different dedications, originally St. Michael the Archangel, St. Mary in 1865, and finally St. Thomas the Apostle in 1875. The building dates mainly from the 14th Century and the tower was heightened and porch added during the 15th Century. The village school was built in 1846 and extended in 1886. It finally closed in 1952 when pupils were transferred to the newly built Langstone school. Redwick school is now a private residence but still retains the old school bell!

217. The interior of St. Thomas's Church Redwick circa 1951. This photograph was taken shortly before the removal of the Victorian screen. However, the rood loft which is some 700 years old, remains and can be seen today. The Church contains many interesting features including a facility for baptism by full immersion, a Norman font and an unusual east window. The Church has over the last few years been subjected to a thorough renovation including the restoration of the Church bells and the addition of a fine Victorian pipe organ.

218. The Rose Inn Redwick with a fair proportion of the Edmonds family posing for the camera in about 1904. At one time the village boasted another pub called The King's Head.

219. Redwick School in 1931. Left to right, back row: Betty Christopher, Tom Moore, Kathleen Cochrane, Alice Stark, Gertie Griffith, Irene Phillips, Grace Monk, Hilda Halfacre and Tom Jones. 2nd row: Courtney Waters, Gwyn Williams, Carrie Lawrence, May Williams, Nora Williams, Clarice Monk, Kathleen Monk and Mostyn Lawrence. 3rd row: Priscilla Christopher, Herbert James, Blanche James, Peggy Lawrence, Pat Lawrence, Morwen Lawrence, Doreen Lewis and Harold Roper. Front row: Bill Lines, Tom Baker, Fred Baker, Will James, Leonard Cochrane, Jim Cochrane, Roy Barnes and Harold Roper.

220. During the years of austerity following the Second World War, the arrival of a new village hall at Redwick was most welcome. Fundraising events were held throughout the 1930's to help build new premises but as more and more people left the district during the depression and with the outbreak of war in 1939, the project was abandoned. Eventually in 1946, the plans were resurrected, thus with £1000 raised by the villagers and £2000 provided by Monmouthshire Rural Community Council, a new hall was constructed. This photograph is from the opening ceremony performed by Sir William J.C. Thomas (Baronet) on August 18th 1949.

REDWICK SPORTS AND OPENING
CEREMONY OF NEW PARISH HALL,

Thursday, August 18th, 1949.

Complimentary Ticket

(Admit to Tea and Sports)

105

With the Compliments of the
Redwick Hall & Sports Committee.

Acknowledgements

Very many people have helped in the production of this book, through their willingness to share information and by the provision of many old photographs.

On occasion it is difficult to determine the 'facts' and any errors that occur, must be considered the author's responsibility for which sincere apologies are offered.

Grateful thanks are due to the undermentioned who kindly loaned original material and who helped to identify faces, places and dates. Apologies are extended to anyone who may have been inadvertently and unintentionally ommitted.

Mrs. Ann Anderson, Mrs. Alice Ashwin, Mrs. Doreen Ball, Mr. Pat Bladon, Rev. Peter Cobb, Mrs. Christine Collingbourne, Mrs. Della David, Mr. Jack Dickenson, Rev. Peter Smallman Edwards, Mrs. Marjorie Evans, Mrs. Gleed, Mr. Ross Goff, Mr. Heurtly Harries, Mr. Paul Hayward, Mr. Gordon Hodges, Mrs. Betty Hopkins, Mr. and Mrs. Archie Jones, Mr. Dave Jones, Miss Olive Lee, Mr. Mark Lewis, Mr. and Mrs. Stan Monk, Mrs. Gwyneth Palmer, Mrs. Barbara Porter, Mr. Peter Strong, Mrs. Dulcie Thomas, Mr. and Mrs. Jim Washbourne, Mr. Ray Washbourne, Mr. and Mrs. David Williams, Mrs. Grace Williams and Mr. Phillip Wood.

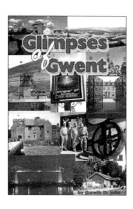
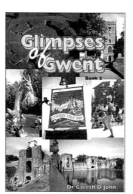
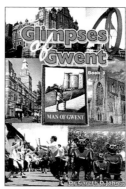
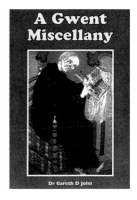

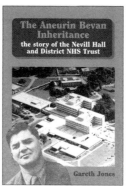

A small selection of many other titles available from Old Bakehouse Publications.